Wise at Any Age
A Handbook for Cultivating Wisdom

Kaitlyn S. C. Hatch

Wise at any Age

ISBN: 978-1-291-43399-9

Author's Blog
www.kaitlynschatch.com

Fancy a chat about the book?
I'm up for a discussion!
@faunawolf on Twitter

Contents

Introduction   4

Defining Wisdom   6

Curiosity   8

Teachers   14

Wisdom Through Observation   20

Wisdom Through Experience   26

Universal Wisdom   32

Tools to Cultivate Wisdom   38

Meditation   40

Mindfulness   44

Coaching or Therapy   50

Discussion   52

Journaling   56

Reading   58

Letting Go & The Power of Doubt   62

We All Have Potential   64

Genuine Gratitude   65

Worth a Thought   66

"What I have to say has all been said before,
And I am destitute of learning and of skill with words.
I therefore have no thought that this might be of benefit to others;
I wrote it only to sustain my understanding"

Shantideva

About the Author

Kaitlyn Hatch is a Buddhist and trained Neuro-Linguistic Programming Practitioner. She's also a Creative Specialist, which is a quick way of saying she's a graphic designer, painter, sculptor, animator and writer.

She's a bit neurotic and appreciates that this gives her a lot to work with.

Introduction

It is often assumed that with age comes wisdom. The phrase 'respect your elders' reflects the understanding that if someone is older than you then they must know better than you. The phrase does not explicitly say why but the belief is that someone who has been there and done that is someone who should automatically be worthy of our respect.

This book presents the idea that wisdom is not necessarily related to the number of experiences a person has had, but instead a reflection of the lessons the person has learned from those experiences. An individual may have a single experience once and learn a profound lesson whilst having another experience a multitude of times and learn nothing.

The age at which we learn a particular life lesson varies greatly as each individual's experience is unique. In my life I have learned invaluable lessons from people half my age and seen astounding foolishness in people twice my age. Nonetheless, that's not to say that those who are older than us have nothing to offer. Statistically the odds are that the more experiences you've had, the more opportunities you've had for growth and therefore, those who reach a certain age *should* be inclined to be wiser than those who have not.

But wisdom is not something that just happens to us and we do not have to wait to cultivate it. Opportunities for wisdom are all around you. They exist in everything you do if you know how to look for them. And we do not have to feel that if we have reached a certain age it is too late to cultivate wisdom.

One of my favourite sayings, possibly of my own invention, although I'm sure it's been said before, is: **Wisdom is not about how many years you have lived but how many lessons you have learned.**

This book is a toolkit for anyone seeking to find the lessons available through their own experiences. Throughout you will find 'tangent' boxes, which are opportunities for you to contemplate, consider and question. There are also drawings, worksheets, and space for making notes. Everyone learns differently so I encourage you to use this book however you see fit.

Much of what I have to say has been said before. That's the thing about wisdom - the lessons are universal even if our experiences are not. In addition to that, we must each find what works best for us.

I'll touch on this in further chapters, but the lesson can only be learned when we are ready for it. It is not enough to read what anyone has written, regardless of their own insights and perspectives. We must be open to doing our own work.

Personal growth is not a solitary endeavor. The act of change comes from within but it's the support of those around us which gives us energy, helps us to be aware and allows us to see a reflection of our actions. Think of this book as a tool but also as a way of connecting to the community around you. Find others who are seeking individual growth, share your thoughts on cultivating wisdom, and please do discuss the things you read on these pages.

Regardless of how you came to have this book in your hands (or on your tablet, in which case you can look up a good note taking app), I want to wish you all the best on your journey. This is just another step, which could illuminate or fall flat, but it's worth trying out. Indeed, cultivation of wisdom is about discovery. So read on and discover.

Defining Wisdom

Before we can look at tools for cultivating wisdom we need to look at the word itself. The English language has so many words and as times have changed so have meanings. We also have our own unique experiences that can determine how we define a word. **My definition and your definition might not match up.** If this book is going to be useful we need to clarify what is meant by wisdom.

Because 'wisdom' is the mass noun of the word 'wise', I'm going to start with that. To be wise is to be considered sensible, prudent and have significant knowledge of a subject, idea or body of work. To have wisdom is to possess the qualities of having experience, knowledge, and good judgement.

In both these definitions the word AND is used rather than OR when listing the qualities of each. So wisdom is not simply having one of these qualities but to possess and demonstrate them collectively.

To gain further clarity let's look at the word 'intelligence'. Intelligence is defined as the ability to acquire skills and knowledge. Wisdom and intelligence go hand in hand, but I want to put out some real clarity on how wisdom will be used within this book.

Intelligence is the ability we have to learn new things. We can go about this in many ways but ultimately intelligence is about what we know and our ability to add to what we know.

Wisdom is the ability we have to act sensibly, with discernment, based on what we know through experience, thought, meditation, contemplation and discussion.

An intelligent person knows something. **A wise person knows what to do with that knowledge.**

Tangent Box

Let's examine how definitions differ by looking at the word 'judgement'. This can be a pretty loaded word.

Write down what it means to you:

Now look it up in a dictionary and compare your definition to what you find there.

What differences do you notice?

Do you think your own definition is a more accurate reflection of how the word is used today?

What about the context in which it can be used, like having clouded judgement or good judgement?

Curiosity

The world is a big place but thanks to developing technology we are more connected than ever. This is, possibly, a loose use of the word 'connected' as it's difficult to say how in touch we are with one another when our communication is conducted primarily through texting, for example. But I digress.

What I'm getting at is that we know a lot more about the world around us than ever before. We are more aware of the things going on in other countries or even things going on in our own country. We are now exposed to a multitude of different cultures, ideas, and teachings.

It can be easy to look at the state of the world and say that it's worse off than it has ever been, but this wouldn't be a true statement. The world is, and always has been, balanced. There is equal attribution of positive and negative throughout. The difference is, we hear about things faster and from more sources than ever before.

Tangent Box

Handy space for your thoughts on the subject:

When someone says 'The world is worse now than it's ever been' do you agree or disagree?

What evidence do you look at to come up with your opinion about this statement?

If you had to present an argument one way or another, what examples or resources would you use?

But with fast communication comes a potentially great risk: Fast miscommunication.

Something untrue or out of context can spread quickly, causing great damage in its wake. Most people aren't going to source check. They simply tweet, post it on their wall, email it on to friends and perpetuate a viral spread of misinformation. A classic and sometimes amusing example of this is quotes on the Internet. My favourite is "The problem with quotes on the Internet is, it's hard to verify their authenticity", attributed to Abraham Lincoln.

I was an inquisitive kid. I would bombard my parents with question after question, my curiosity seemingly insatiable. I'm not sure if she got bored of it or she was actually trying to encourage me to find stuff out for myself, but my mum's approach was to encourage me to look up answers to my questions. "Go get a dictionary. That's what it's for."

This was in the days before the Internet. In my home we had an encyclopedia, a dictionary, medical dictionary and multiple other reference books. We went to the library frequently and I was able to access good old Microfiche, the library computer system and other tools which could be used to answer my questions.

An inquisitive and questioning mind is something essential to the development of wisdom.

Oftentimes the role of an educational institution can become muddled. There might be the belief that schools are there to help us become good citizens or to develop our social skills. They can be said to exist to give us a basic understanding of the world in which we live as a platform for further discovery. It is true that they certainly do provide these things, but at the very core of it, an educational institution that has succeeded is one that inspires its students to be inquisitive and figure stuff out.

A friend of mine once said, "The role of a teacher, and the role of a school, is to teach people how to learn, how to discover and how to gain more knowledge."

As children, we do have a certain sense of wonder and awe with regards to the world around us. But that curious wonder can weaken with time and does, in some people, disappear entirely. A person can become complacent.

The danger of complacency is that we no longer make up our mind but instead just go along with what every one else is doing, or what we think everyone else is doing. In this way we become sheeple.

Sheeple go with the flow. Sheeple hold a belief based on what everyone else in the group believes. Sheeple don't question an idea, research a source or compare an experience against their own sense of reason.

Being a sheeple isn't always dangerous. A lot of the time it can just make a person look foolish, more than anything.

But sometimes a sheeple mentality can be really harmful. A classic example of harmful sheeple action is the spread of rumours. For example, sheeple mentality on the Internet has led to some decent, hard working people being slandered because of the fast spread of misinformation by a lot of people eager to forward something on without first researching all the facts.

Being aware of ourselves and our own sense of reason, fostering curiosity and seeking to determine our own answers are essential steps to cultivating wisdom. When we are aware of ourselves we cease to be a sheeple and start to be an individual. As an individual we have a greater awareness of our own sense of self, where we fit in the world, and what we believe. When we see things as an individual, rather than from a sheeple perspective, we can be more discerning and considered with our approach.

When you figure something out for yourself through your own process, there is a great sense of satisfaction and accomplishment. There is also more strength in it, because it's not something you were told but something about which you made up your own mind.

Hmm, one in seven people you meet is actually several ducks in a costume. Well! They wouldn't publish it if it wasn't true!

Tangent Box

"Everyone knows that human beings only use 10% of their brain and a goldfish only has a 3 second memory…"

These and other so called 'facts' are wide spread and often repeated without considering where they came from or what studies might have been done to confirm that they are true. As it is, neither of these is true and there is a wealth of proof - if you're curious enough to go looking for it.

Worksheet

Political speeches are designed to get the audience engaged by promoting a sense of enthusiasm and excitement. It's all about change! Something different! An improvement over the other parties!

Most political speeches are written for sheeple. They are designed to appeal to the masses and in this way most of them hardly say anything at all.

In this worksheet you're invited to do a quick online search of political speeches (there are whole archive sites of political speeches from almost every country in the world) and pick one to read through. Be discerning, be critical, and note how much of the speech is actually telling you something and how much of it is non-specific.

Because this book is a toolkit I've provided space for you to make notes and write questions or general thoughts, if that's a way of learning that works for you. If you're using an e-reader or tablet, this is one of those times a note app might come in handy.

Teachers

When I was in school I was frequently told by peers and teachers alike that most people will only ever have one great teacher in their lifetime. I disagreed with this and still do because it simply doesn't match up with my own experience, nor the experience of many of the people I've met. First of all, teachers come in many forms and many different contexts.

A teacher isn't necessarily a person who stands at the front of a literal classroom. A teacher can be our friend who is always late or our family member who doesn't really listen. These people teach us the importance of patience and clear communication.

Tangent Box

Handy space for your thoughts on the subject:

Do you agree? How many significant teachers can you list in your own life?

A teacher can also be someone we really dislike. The people who cause us grief or get under our skin or really irritate us are the very same people who show us where we have to grow. They are the ones who keep our egos in check. When we think we're doing really well at being compassionate, kind, caring and wise a difficult person is bound to show up and show us up. They are humbling for the character.

And then there are the teachers who speak a truth that you already know but possibly haven't been able to put into words. For example, I had been seeing a psychologist for some time and in our discussions she often mentioned that a lot of what I was saying was very Buddhist. She would specifically say that I sounded a lot like Pema Chodron and the things she teaches.

I eventually got around to researching Buddhism properly (having taken a surface look at it as a teenager) and buying one of Pema's books. I did not choose to be a Buddhist so much as I had the realisation that I always had been a Buddhist. It took the right teachers (my psychologist and Pema) at the right time to make me realise that there was a teaching, philosophy and belief system that fit me like a glove.

Not every teacher we meet is obvious at the time. It may be well after the fact that we realise someone helped us to learn a valuable lesson and therefore cultivate greater wisdom. I say 'helped us to learn' because ultimately, what we discover is up to us. Which brings me to the most important teacher in your life:

You

You are your own most important teacher because it is up to you what lessons you learn, how you learn them, when and why. The choice is yours, even if you are currently unconscious of it.

When we cultivate wisdom we become more and more aware of ourselves and the decisions we make. We then become more conscious of our choices, actions, and beliefs. To be our own greatest teacher we must learn to make up our own minds. We do this by gathering all the information we need (being curious, asking questions) and using our own sense of reasoning to determine what fits for us.

Tangent Box

Reading Pema's writing was like having a big 'Aha!' moment.

Can you think of a time when you've been reading something written by someone else and it matched your own beliefs so well you felt it might as well have been written by your own hand?

Worksheet

We can learn a lot from someone we admire or look up to, but some of the greatest teachers in my life have been those who have gotten on my nerves, irritated me, or generally caused me a sense of frustration.

These experiences are an opportunity to practice patience, generosity, and compassion. They can make us aware of our own limitations, like when we defer the responsibility of how we feel to another person, rather than looking at our own propensities and what triggers them.

In this worksheet I invite you to think of one or two individuals who have challenged you.

Perhaps there's a co-worker or manager that you had a lot of conflict with. Maybe a family member that seems to cause a lot of drama. A friend who is draining of your time and energy.

What did you learn about yourself from your relationship with them?

How have you changed?

If you meet someone similar, how will you behave or treat them differently?

19

Wisdom Through Observation

When I was twelve I had a friend whose parents fought a lot. It was a difficult year for her because she was pretty sure they were going to get divorced. She didn't want her family to split up. She also felt really alone with her worry as her brother, bless him, slept like the dead and didn't hear the fights. She did, however, and she paid attention to what she heard and would confide her worries in me.

As with many relationships the root cause of the problem was money. There simply wasn't enough. She didn't know the details but her parents were willing to do the work to find a solution that not only saved their relationship but very likely made it stronger than ever.

The solution was two-fold:
1. Her mum wanted to go back to work and did within a short period of time.
2. Her parents began giving themselves an allowance. This was a monthly amount they each got which they could do with as they pleased without needing to consult the other because this was over and above what was allotted to bill payments.

Here was the opportunity for two lessons:
1. It is important for us to maintain our individuality, even when we are in a relationship. ie. There is no such thing as 'another half'. Be your own whole person.
2. It is important to have a sense of financial independence.

As it was, my friend learned the second lesson through observation alone. She was able to see how her parents found a solution, applied it, and resolved the issue around finances. She didn't have to live it to learn it.

The risk, however, in using the experiences of others to cultivate our own wisdom is that we will adopt received or 'blind' wisdom.

Received wisdom isn't actually wisdom at all. Received wisdom includes 'Old wives' tales' - things handed on without actually checking the source. There's a joke that illustrates this quite well.

A young woman is preparing a roast for dinner. She cuts the ends off and her husband asks her why. She replies, "Well, my mother always cut the ends off."
"Why did she do it?"
"It's supposed to make it taste better."
"How?"
The woman is confounded so she calls up her mum to ask. Her mum says, "Your grandmother always cut the ends off."
So the woman hangs up and calls her grandmother and asks her why she cut the ends off.
"So it would fit in my little roasting pan," her grandmother says.

Received wisdom is when we accept what someone tells us without weighing it against our own experience.

When I was a kid, my brother really, really hated onions. He said they were revolting things with a weird texture. I admired him a lot and so I refused to eat onions too, even though I'd not tried them for myself.

One day my family played a game at dinner where we all pretended to be a different member of the family. My dad played me, my mum played my brother, my brother played my dad and I played my mum. I was about seven or eight. My dad had onions on his plate and true to my character he pushed them to the very edge and made a face. I loved acting and was going to be very true to my mum so I offered to eat his onions, just as my mum often did for my brother or me.

They were delicious. I hadn't realised how delicious something could be. In fact, I love onions so much that I often go through eight in a week. If you were to offer me a chocolate bar or a fried onion I would take the onion every time. That's how much I love onions.

Received wisdom can be quite harmless, as illustrated in the above story. But it pays to question it because sometimes received wisdom can actually be quite harmful. Basing a belief on the experience of another person can narrow your own view of the world.

In communities or families where a feeling of hatred is fostered towards another group of people, racism, sexism, ageism, transphobia, ableism, homophobia or classism will grow. None of us are born believing that some humans are less valuable or worthy of respect than others.

Wisdom certainly can be gained through listening or observing the actions of a person or group of people, but we must still put our observations through our own filters to ensure that we are not blindly following a belief.

Worksheet

We don't always learn from watching the actions of others, but sometimes the lesson is more clear to an outsider than it is to the person actually experiencing it. Think of how often you've seen a miscommunication between friends or colleagues. They may have been completely unaware of what was being missed while you were able to see exactly where things went wrong.

The ability to see clearly helps anyone seeking to cultivate wisdom. By noticing what others miss we can begin to see where we can get muddled too.

If you can, think of a time when you've witnessed a miscommunication and what it was that allowed you to notice the disconnect between those directly involved.

If nothing comes to mind use the next week as an experiment to see how often this might happen, if at all. Use the worksheet space to record your thoughts or observations on our ability to see clearly when we are viewing something from the outside.

Wisdom Through Experience

Our experiences make up the person we are and because experience is constantly changing we are constantly changing. Experience is an interesting thing because there is the actual thing that happened and then there is our understanding and memory of it.

Two people will experience the exact same situation in two different ways. Because of this, two people can also learn two entirely different lessons from the same situation.

There have been many studies on eye-witness testimony which illustrate this beautifully. To explore this further you can look up Loftus and Palmer's (1974) reconstruction of automobile destruction , Lipton's (1977) study of eyewitness testimony, and Cutler et al's (1989) look at the unreliability of eyewitness testimony.

Five people who witness the same crime taking place can have five different descriptions of what happened. This is because we all view the world through our own filters based on our personal experience.

Tangent Box

Handy space for your thoughts on the subject:

An opinion is a view or judgement formed about something. Because our opinions are based on our experiences, they cannot be 'right' or 'wrong'. They can be informed or misinformed but not 'right' or 'wrong' because an opinion is entirely personal.

When we cultivate wisdom through our experience it's important to remember that this is going to be unique to us. We can always discuss with others, share our thoughts or ask for opinions, but ultimately what we discover or how we grow after a particular situation is going to be down to us.

That's not to say we always learn the lesson. When something seems to come up repeatedly it's easy to fall into a victim mentality of thinking the world is out to get us or we just have really bad luck.

Life is not out to get us. Life is entirely indifferent. When the same thing keeps arising it's a chance for us to look at opportunities for growth. If we don't, the situation will keep arising until we get it right.

A great example of this is in the people we meet in our lives. We have friends, family members, neutral people like our postman or bus driver, co-workers, employers, etc. Some people might play a very supportive role in our lives and be around for a long time. Others may come and go for a multitude of reasons. Within many of them we will see similarities.

We're all familiar with meeting someone new and feeling like we've known them our whole lives, or comparing them to someone else in our life who shares the same energy or attitude as them. We might meet someone who reminds us of a family member who is supportive of us. There's a sort of similar energy going on and in this way we are open and receptive to getting to know them better.

Then there are those times when we meet someone and there's something a bit off-putting about them. We might not be able to put our finger on it but something about that person brings up a feeling of aversion in us.

Most people will be quite open to the person who brings up feelings of fondness and well being in them while being closed down to someone for whom they feel aversion. It's a natural part of being human - we like to push away things we don't like and hold onto things we do like.

Of course this push and pull doesn't always work and our aversion is a chance for us to pay attention.

I had an employer for whom I had a great dislike. She rubbed me the wrong way and there was a lot about her attitude and action in the world that conflicted with my own common sense and good judgement. I was discussing this with my psychologist when she stopped me and asked me who this employer reminded me of. I thought about it for a moment and realised that they were very similar to a previous employer I'd had. Both had, in my opinion, been self-serving and manipulative. Both had a loose work ethic and were rarely punctual.

But there were some key differences. I had lacked confidence when I'd been employed by the first and had not stood up for myself when I should have. With this new troublemaker, I was far more assertive and wouldn't let her take advantage of me.

However, I was still struggling. There was still room for growth since this troublemaker had popped up again, albeit in a different form.

The thing about our experience is that things will inevitably keep coming up until we do the work needed. I am still on the lookout for that troublemaker in yet a different form because I don't know that I've learned all the lessons that I can from them.

Certainly, I've learned to be assertive, to walk away from employment where I feel I am perpetuating or contributing to something immoral, to say "No" when asked to do things beyond my job description, and that I am allowed to ask for a pay increase that is commensurate with my performance.

The thing I must remember, that we all must remember, is that we cannot change other people. It's not possible for us to change someone else. Only they can do that. When cultivating wisdom through our interactions with those around us we have to start with ourselves, where we are at the moment. Often times we will realise that something we dislike about someone else is actually something we dislike, or are worried about, within ourselves.

When we stop trying to change someone else we can become aware of these projections. Then we can start working on ourselves, instead of trying to change the actions or behaviours of those around us.

Worksheet

When I was little my mum and I would clash quite often because I liked to test boundaries and I was very stubborn.

"You make me so angry!" I would shout.

"I don't make you angry. You choose to feel angry," came my mum's infuriating reply.

I was a child and all I knew was that I was upset, angry and hurt after my mum had said something I disagreed with. For the longest time I didn't understand what she could possibly mean because the proof of cause and effect was so blatant to me.

She said something, I got angry. Clearly she was 'making' me angry.

I eventually came to understand what she meant when I began to understand our propensities. A propensity is our inclination to behave or react in a certain way. Usually this is based on doing what we have always done in the past.

When we pay attention to our propensities we have the opportunity to change them, if we choose. For example, as a teenager I had the propensity to feel anxious and afraid if a bully approached me in the hallway. I would see other people who didn't have this reaction and one day I started to change my behaviour - even though I still felt the same anxiety - by standing up to the bullies and asking them why they were saying something mean or hurtful.

Eventually I no longer had the propensity to feel anxious when I saw a bully approaching. Instead I felt assertive and confident that I could defend myself.

What are some examples of propensities you have been able to change or shed?

Universal Wisdom

Do your research and you'll soon discover that there is a certain universality to wisdom. Look at the words and teachings of Gandhi, The Dalai Lama, Helen Keller or Nelson Mandela. All of them have pretty much the same message:

BE AWARE OF OTHERS

DO TO OTHERS AS YOU WOULD EXPECT TO BE DONE TO YOURSELF

WE ALL HAVE UNLIMITED POTENTIAL FOR GREATNESS

PRACTICE COMPASSION

They all have different religious beliefs, different backgrounds and come from different countries. They are just three examples of thousands available to us when we get curious and do our research.

An awareness of universal wisdom shows us that there are core truths about the world we live in which will continue to arise generation after generation. How we discover these truths is part of our individual path and is going to be entirely up to us.

Tangent Box

Handy space for your thoughts on the subject:

All four of the individuals mentioned are well known for their political activism and fighting for social change. They are also known for being exceptionally kind, generous and genuine.

In the face of great adversity they remain positive and open - even to those who have oppressed them. What does this tell you about the nature of Universal Wisdom?

We may have an experience which seems insignificant at first, but leads us to a valuable lesson about shared humanity. The thing is, these lessons are there for us when we need them and everyone has the same opportunity to learn them, if they are looking.

Using the term 'lesson' might cloud things a bit so I want to discuss the essence of universal wisdom.

A core truth is an indisputable fact about the nature of reality. Cultivating wisdom is about learning to see the world as it is, without story lines. It's about recognising the nature of reality and the role we play in it, both as individuals and collectively.

When we study in school we are being taught how to find things out. We are also being taught how to find out the correct answer. When it comes to wisdom though, right/wrong thinking doesn't really work. It's not about seeing what is 'right' or 'wrong' but seeing what *is*, plain and simple.

To illustrate this let us take a look at the phrase: Life isn't fair.

Fairness is held in high regard by the human race. Fairness is about getting what you deserve, especially if you have been 'good'. But we all know that life throws us curveballs. Regardless of upbringing, belief system, family background, personal values and so on, we will all experience loss, disappointment, pain, grief, and other forms of suffering.

As a race of storytellers we feel the need to have a bad guy, a clear plot, and reason behind the things that happen to us.

But it's true: Life isn't fair.

Tangent Box

Handy space for your thoughts on the subject:

Where do you think the expectation that life should be 'fair' comes from?

Life isn't anything. Life just is. It happens. The very birth of the Universe is an example of the spontaneity and unpredictability of the world in which we live. Universal wisdom comes from an awareness of this whole phenomenon and an understanding that what we see as 'good' and 'bad' are a reflection of our own personal experience, not a reflection of reality.

It's important, when looking at universal wisdom, not to get it mixed up with the received wisdom mentioned previously. Received wisdom is something like, "Women are not as valuable as men and therefore are not considered to be equal." This was, once, quite widely believed, but one can quickly differentiate between this and universal wisdom, which expounds equality for all. Take away the story lines and the history and even when it was a universally held belief that women were less valuable than men, it was not a reflection of the true nature of reality.

Of course the most important thing to remember is, even universal wisdom should be filtered through your own sense of reason.

Worksheet

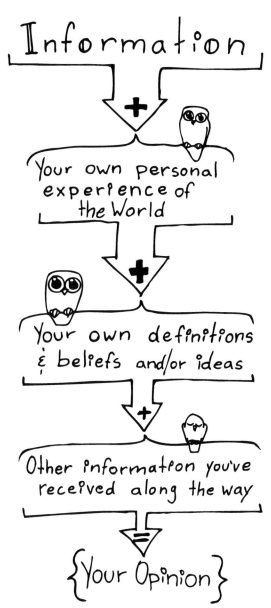

Information

+

Your own personal experience of the World

+

Your own definitions & beliefs and/or ideas

+

Other information you've received along the way

={Your Opinion}

Universal wisdom is often quite abstract or very general. A universal wisdom will be applied differently in the lives of each individual who has considered it.

Take a look at the 'Golden Rule': Do unto others as you would have them do unto you.

How might different people apply the idea that you should treat others as you would have others treat you in their lives?

How do you choose to apply it in your own life, if at all?

What might this phrase mean if you are extremely negative and critical towards or have a low opinion of yourself?

Tools to Cultivate Wisdom

At the start of this book wisdom was defined as our ability to act sensibly, with discernment, based on what we know through experience, thought, meditation, contemplation and discussion.

To have an experience is not enough to gain wisdom from it. The mere act of existing long enough doesn't make us wise.

Tangent Box

Handy space for your thoughts on the subject:

Do you agree with the statement that how long we've lived doesn't neccesarily reflect how wise we are?

It's what we do with what we know that allows us to become wiser. But how to go about this isn't always easy. Lessons aren't necessarily obvious and many of us spend a lot of time filling up our lives with distractions and missing what's happening right now, in the moment.

Think of wisdom as a seed in a pot. Before it can grow, it needs the right conditions. To thrive it needs nutrients, water, and sun. We are all full of little seeds of wisdom waiting for the right conditions.

Sometimes the conditions can arise all on their own. We will have a particular experience and be receptive to a lesson it has to offer. But we don't have to wait around. We can create the right conditions to feed our wisdom.

This is part of being your own greatest teacher. You can set up the conditions because you value yourself enough to do so. Just like a gardener values the potential of that little seed, you value the potential you have to live wisely.

You may already have some great tools and feel that you are an expert at setting up the right conditions. In that case, brilliant! Carry on! And if you want you can use this bit for notes to write down the things you already do.

Perhaps you have a few ideas but aren't entirely sure what works. Or maybe you've been trying some things but they've not been working at all. Or you hadn't even considered the idea of creating the right conditions.

In the next chapters are just a few ideas, but remember, test things out and find out what works for you. Don't do anything unless it agrees with your own sense of reason.

Meditation

The primary purpose of meditation is to cultivate wisdom.

There are several different types of meditation including Mindfulness, Metta, Tonglen, and Zen. If you're new to meditation there are quite a few ways you can go about learning more. Here's where your curiosity can help you.

You could start by looking into the different kinds of meditation. See which one initially takes your fancy.

There are many introductory meditation classes or sessions you could attend. These can be found at Buddhist centres or through holistic clinics. A quick online search will pull up a multitude of options. Do your research into what is offered as there are many forms of meditation, each one with a slightly different focus.

You could get a book or CD about meditation which include guided practices. I personally recommend anything by Pema Chodron or Sharon Salzberg, but again, do your research. The teacher can be as important as the lesson.

The following are some myths about meditation which I commonly encounter. They may or may not help you to understand why meditation is used as a tool to cultivate wisdom.

MYTH: Meditation is relaxing - Anyone who has done any amount of meditation knows this isn't true. The actual act of sitting still and focusing on the breath is a challenge. Our bodies can grow uncomfortable and weary even when our posture is right. Our minds are also a general whirlwind. Thoughts arise on their own and the act of 'not thinking' is far more challenging than most realise.

In fact, to meditate effectively, you must create a sense of relaxation prior to sitting. It is a good practice to allow some time - five minutes even - before sitting down to meditate to come into your body and relax your mind. Repeating phrases such as, "I am here now, and nothing needs to be done" or taking five to ten deep, deliberate breaths are great ways to calm the mind and body and prepare for meditation.

MYTH: Meditation is blissful - Not true. Meditation is a practice done to cultivate wisdom. We meditate to focus the mind and in doing so gain a more resourceful state. A resourceful state is merely a state in which we are able to act effectively, rather than irrationally or with strong emotion. A resourceful state is any state in which we perform at our best.

When we meditate we focus the mind and experience the state we are in at that very moment. We free ourselves from the distraction of the past or the future or any story lines we may be holding onto. In any given moment we could be experiencing a range of feelings from calm to anxious, happiness to anger. Meditation allows us to sit with our experience rather than being averse to it or clinging to it.

For anyone who has ever sat with their anxiety, anger, sadness or any other feeling commonly referred to as 'bad', the feeling is not one of bliss. It can actually be quite scary to sit with an emotion which makes us uncomfortable but in doing so we can recognise that emotions are as fleeting as our thoughts. They come and go, ebb and flow, just like waves in the ocean.

MYTH: Meditation will 'fix' you - I don't believe that people are broken. People can be confused, oblivious, in turmoil, struggling, frustrated, neurotic and so on, but these states are not broken states. They are simply unresourceful states which can make life seem challenging to lead.
The purpose of meditation is not to 'repair' anything but to learn to accept what is. Meditation is an exploration of the self.

Many of us do whatever we can to ignore or avoid the things about ourselves which we don't like. We can use any manner of distraction. I used to throw myself into work or into 'fixing' other people in order to avoid working on my own stuff. Through meditation I became acutely aware of this fact.

At first, seeing ourselves for who we are and all the things we do, even the things we are averse to, is actually quite disheartening. It can be crushing to our spirit to think that we are not put-together, well-adjusted beings.

But meditation is not just about being able to see where we are still growing or in need of change, it's about embracing the fact that we are flawed. Even if we obtain enlightenment we will always be flawed. An enlightened being recognises that their flaws are part of them just like anything else. Flaws do not define us but they do contribute to who we are as individuals.

Meditation allows us to make friends with ourselves, warts and all, and in doing so we learn to let go of those things which are not beneficial to our growth.

Now, some truths about meditation:

TRUTH: Meditation can be done anywhere. You can meditate on the train, in a park, or during your lunch break. It's about being present in mind and body, which is a good habit to get into even when you're not sitting in a quiet room by yourself.

TRUTH: Meditation doesn't have to be time consuming. There is no limit to how long you can sit for but it's good to try to take at least ten minutes, just to allow yourself time to get into a meditative state. Finding ten minutes out of your day for meditation is pretty easy if you are looking for it and willing to try.

TRUTH: Everyone can meditate. Anyone can do it, regardless of their culture, social status, age, upbringing, gender, sexuality, ability, height, hair colour, taste in clothing - you get the idea. People who meditate don't belong to a special club or have special abilities or skills. It's not mysterious or inaccessible.

You could give it a go right now. Sit in a position where your posture is good. Your spine should be straight as though someone were holding you up by a string pulled from the top of you head. Make sure you have a solid base, either in a chair with your feet flat on the ground or sitting on a cushion on the floor so that you don't wobble. It's best to try to avoid crossing anything as limbs can quickly go numb and you'll soon just be meditating about how sore or tingly that feels!

As soon as you're comfortable you can either close your eyes or leave them open ever so slightly - gazing downwards two or three feet ahead of you. Then take a moment to become aware of your breath. Notice how it feels as it passes over the edge of your nostrils or, if your mouth is open, the parting of your lips. Does it go into your chest or down into your belly? Is it slow or fast? Don't try to control it - just notice it.

And that's it! You're meditating.

Mindfulness

Mindfulness is a result of meditation but something you can practice on its own as well. Some people might disagree with me on this, which is great and why we're such a wonderful interesting bunch of creatures. If you disagree I've put a little note section where you can write down why.

Mindfulness is the ability to be aware. This is an all encompassing awareness. Practicing mindfulness can be quite challenging when you start and even when you've been doing it for several years. In fact, mindfulness can prove to be a near impossible task when you become aware of just how unaware we tend to be.

To be mindful is to refrain from distraction. The opposite is mindlessness. When we are mindless (not thoughtless) we seek distraction. We watch television, go on Facebook, type out 140 characters in the hope that someone will distract us. Mindlessness is like chewing up your food and spitting it out without swallowing it. We get the flavour of what we put in our mouths but we wasted all the nutrients, vitamins, and other benefits we would have had if we'd swallowed.

Tangent Box

Handy space for your thoughts on the subject:

If mindfulness is about paying attention to your experience, and thoughtfulness is being considerate of other people's experience, how do you think being 'thoughtless' is different from not being mindful?

My first introduction to mindfulness was during a session with my psychologist. She got me to eat a raisin. The first thing was simply to pick the raisin from the bag. To feel it in my fingers. I held it for some time, over a minute, just being aware of the texture of it. Where the skin was smooth or wrinkled. How it felt a bit soft but the skin was firm. Where there was a sharpness on one end where the stem hadn't been entirely removed.

The next step was to hold it to my mouth, under my nose, against my lips. To experience any sensations that way. To feel and smell it. she got me to close my eyes as well, so I could be aware of other senses beyond my sight.

When I finally put it in my mouth, probably a full three minutes after I'd picked it up, I just held it there. I became aware of the shape of it in my mouth but also aware of my reaction to it. I began to salivate and my tongue danced around it.

She instructed me to bite it, but only once, and observe the feelings that came after that. I got the taste of it, the sugars rushing down my throat. A clenching desire to swallow.

I chewed it very slowly, remaining aware of all the sensations that accompany the eating of a single raisin. By the time I'd finished it had taken me just over five minutes from the time I'd picked it up to the time I finally swallowed the last traces of it.

She asked me what I thought about eating a raisin that way and I laughed. "I've often eaten raisins that way."

Since I was a kid I'd enjoyed eating raisins very slowly. I liked to peeled the skin from the sugary, soft inside using my teeth and tongue. I'd cram the gooey interiors into one cheek, slowly finishing off the skin and swallowing that. It was even more fun when I had a chocolate covered raisin as there was the added step of very slowly sucking all the chocolate off of it.

Mindfulness is not a new idea for any of us. We all know what it feels like because we all have things which we enjoy doing mindfully because it feels natural to us.

Making a puzzle is a great example of a mindful activity. For those who enjoy assembling them they know that sensation of being completely absorbed in the task at hand, focusing on the shape, feel and colour of each piece to form the picture on the box.

When we learn something new, like how to drive a car or ride a bike, we tend to be very mindful. Our awareness of what we do not know is heightened and therefore we are more focused on our actions. We pay attention to each step required to balance and pedal or shift and accelerate.

Mindfulness is the act of paying attention and living in the moment. It's the act of actually being present.

Most of the time we are not present. We are distracted by the past or thinking ahead to the future. We worry, fret, and regret rather than just being with what is right at that moment.

When we practice mindfulness we learn to become present and when we can be present we are aware of all aspects of a situation. When someone is doing an activity mindfully, like working out, gardening, or building a lego structure, they are aware of how they are right then.

Being aware of how you are in any given moment is extremely beneficial. When we are aware of our experience we can look at it with reason. When we are able to be reasonable, to be aware of our state, we can make more wise choices and learn from the experience as it is happening rather than tainting it with past memories or future ideas.

Being mindful isn't about ignoring past experiences or not planning for the future. It's not a matter of not doing one thing in favour of another. Being mindful is simply appreciating your current experience as it is the only thing you have to work with. We can only work with what is right now. Sometimes how we work with it will be influenced by what we have learned before but sometimes it's worth taking an experience as it is with an open mind and heart.

Being mindful is also a great way to appreciate the time we have in a day. When you conduct yourself in a mindful way you might be surprised at how many hours you fritter away doing mindless activities.

I experienced this when I attended a meditation retreat. There were no distractions: No television, computers, smart phones, even regular phones. Even the book I'd brought was one about meditation and personal insight, so not a fiction adventure for me to get lost in.

Tangent Box

There's nothing wrong with indulging in distraction. It's only when we use distraction to avoid dealing with what's really going on that it can cause problems.

When we ignore something that's bringing up strong emotions in us we risk making it worse. Just like a cold won't get any better if we don't take care of ourselves, our mental health suffers when we numb ourselves to emotions we deem unpleasant or 'negative'. Do you agree?

By the end of my week I realised how much time I spend distracting myself with the Internet, texting, and 'busy-work' - when I sort of flit about the house fussing over things but not really getting anything done.

I was amazed as I've always thought of myself as a pretty switched on and productive individual. In fact, I like to say that I'm allergic to procrastination.

Being mindful allows us to see where we still have work to do. When we are aware we start to realise that even the things we think we've got sorted might need some work. We can also recognise how those around us might see our actions.

In this way we can also cultivate compassion, along with wisdom, because we can see how all human beings, even those of us who practice mindfulness, can be quite mindless sometimes. In fact, my psychologist likes to say that the only difference between a mindful person and a mindless person is that a mindful person **appreciates** that they don't always know what they do.

Ways to practice mindfulness:

Mindful eating practice - You can use a raisin if you like. In fact, if you don't like raisins then it's a really good practice. But it's also great to do with something you really, really love which you find difficult to eat slowly. Chocolate, for example, is something that many people find very difficult to resist.

Set a timer for five to ten minutes depending on the size of what you're eating - although it's better to use something smaller. So if you are using chocolate just use a single square rather than an entire bar.

Start with touch and sight. Move on to smell. Then taste. Try it with your eyes open for part of the time and closed for others. Be aware of all aspects of the experience - not just the food you are eating but all the sensations in your body as well.

Mindful activity - Anything you can do and be fully present for is a mindful activity. Mindful activities can include but are not limited to:

rowing drawing model assembly
doing the dishes knitting sculpting walking
gardening meditation making a puzzle
photography painting writing cycling
playing an instrument sewing carving
swimming quilting

Coaching or Therapy

A commonly taught lesson in psychology is the act of projection. This is based on the understanding that if we are what we think, and what we think influences how we see the world, then our view of the world is a reflection of our inner selves. This might sound like a bad thing but let us remember the importance of not labeling something as good or bad. It's merely something which is and given that, it's something we can use to our advantage.

Therapy or coaching is a relationship where projection and self reflection are the whole point. The job of a good therapist or coach is to see their client for who they actually are, to the best of their ability. The role of the client is to use the therapist or coach as a reflection so they can look at an issue in an entirely different way.

Tangent Box

Handy space for your thoughts on the subject:

I like to define therapy as something done to **deconstruct** an issue and coaching as the **construction** of something to work with. What do you think? What are the differences between seeing a business or life coach and seeing a counsellor or psychologist?

Of course this isn't something that works for everyone and it's important not to settle. Both the client and the coach or therapist must feel that the relationship is mutually beneficial or it simply won't work. Shopping around is encouraged and it's okay to fire a coach.

When cultivating wisdom it can help immensely to have someone impartial to talk to. Finding a good coach or therapist who fills this role is a very personal thing. For some people coaching or therapy simply won't work. Or maybe coaching does but therapy doesn't or vice versa.

Testing this out is a great way to recognise what your path is. I went to loads of therapists before I found a good fit but I persevered because I knew that an impartial third party worked for me. Even though I'd not found one that worked on a long term, I knew full well that it was a good tool for me to have.

Discussion

Following coaching or therapy is discussion. By sharing our thoughts or ideas, hearing what other people have to say on a subject, and being open to hearing differing opinions and how people came to have them, we broaden our perspective. Discussion allows us to see the sameness we might share with someone as well as the individual paths we take toward enlightenment.

When partaking in discussion to cultivate wisdom it's important to have good listening skills. The more discussion we get involved in the better we will become at listening.

You've probably been bombarded with tips on how to listen. There are books and programs on it and it's usually included in most professional development orientation and training processes.

That's because we're actually quite terrible at listening. My mum used to say, "You'll have to tell a child to do something as many times as you have to tell them until they start doing it."

Whether you're a child or not, reminders are a great thing to help us find our own middle way. Listening is an excellent tool and a key part of a good discussion. When we listen we are doing everything we can to understand the experience of the person talking. We are taking in what they have to say and trying, as best as we can, to understand *their* experience of the world.

In this way we can open up to compassion and strengthen our understanding of each other.

Of course discussion goes both ways. As well as being good listeners we must work on our own communication. It's important to remember that the person or people we are discussing with have their own map of the world, their own experiences and their own ways of defining the language they are using. We must not assume that the people we speak to define 'judgement' or 'happiness' in the same way.

We listen to better understand the experience of those around us and we communicate clearly to better express our own experience.

Tangent Box

As a Canadian I use terms and phrases differently from an American or someone from the UK. For example, one day I was watching a programme with my partner, who happens to be English. One of the people on the show used the word 'homely' to describe something.

I rolled my eyes and said, "They meant 'homey' - people always seem to use the wrong word. They keep putting an 'L' in it." My partner was confused and asked me what I was going on about.

I explained that, because they were talking about a nice, warming soup they'd eaten, they should have said it was a 'homey soup' - as in a home comfort.

My partner continued to be confused though and explained that that's what homely meant so it was perfectly acceptable.

As a Canadian I would only use 'homely' to describe something that was ugly or not very pleasant to look at.

This is just one of so many examples where language - even a common language - can have different meanings to different people.

Tools for wise discussion:

• Get clarity: If you don't understand something or you think you might be misinterpreting it, ask for clarification. Use phrases like, "Can you be specific about what you mean when you say _____?" or "In what context do you mean _____?"

• Paraphrase: Check that you're paying attention to and understanding what has been said by repeating back what has been said in your own words. This is a great way to see how people use words or phrases to mean different things.

• Drop your tongue: This is a technique that has been used by Buddhist monks for hundreds of years. You can test it by sitting very still, as though you were about to meditate. Pay attention to your mind and how much 'chatter' is going on. Allow yourself time to become aware of any thoughts you are having and then, relax your tongue by letting it drop to the floor of your mouth. Thoughts tend to arise all on their own and they can fill our heads when we're trying to listen to someone. By dropping our tongue the chatter tends to go quiet. Don't worry if it doesn't though. Thoughts are like waves in the ocean. They will happen.

Journaling

One of the reasons discussion and therapy/coaching are so beneficial for cultivating wisdom is because they encourage you to get your ideas, thoughts, and contemplations out of your head. By voicing them they inevitably change because they are no longer based on feeling but also have the resonance of articulation around them.

Writing down your thought process is another great way you can achieve this. I find it particularly helpful when I've got something stuck in my head, going around and around, but I don't have anyone to talk to about it or I'm not ready to talk about it yet. Or it may simply be something I don't want to discuss but I want to work through and keeping it in my head is keeping it going around and around in circles.

Writing it down, either by hand or by typing it on a computer, is a great way to do this. The other added bonuses about journaling is there are no rules and you will be the only person who reads it so you can be entirely uncensored.

A lot of people say they would like to keep a journal but can't because they don't have the time or they worry that they wouldn't know how. The beauty of a personal journal is that how you use it is personal. It's your choice. You decide how often to write, how much to write and how to write it.

Tangent Box

Handy space for your thoughts on the subject:

If you don't want to do something you'll find an excuse. If you want to do something, you'll find a way.

Do you agree?

If you want to come up with a short hand system then go ahead. If you want to create an entire code to write it in you can do that too. You can use pen or pencil or crayon if it suits you. You can keep it on your computer or in a book. It can be lined or unlined. It can be drawn. It can be impeccably neat or so messy it's nearly unreadable. You can glue stuff into it. You can keep it on napkins or scrap paper. You can keep it in a binder. You can keep it forever or you can burn it later.

Journaling doesn't have any rules. Journaling is about reflection and thought. It's about taking the internal dialogue and externalising it. How you do that is entirely up to you.

Reading

Books are wonderful things. At the 2012 Paralympics opening ceremonies in London an entire section was dedicated to the value of books and what they can offer us. Fiction and non-fiction, 'good' literature and 'bad' - the value of the written word is immeasurable.

One of the ways human beings learn is through the act of storytelling. We have been sharing stories since before language as we know it today. Stories were communicated through pictures, symbols and dance. This is how we learn.

Intelligence feeds wisdom. The more we know, the more we discover, the more we have to work with. Books are the modern day cave paintings or tribal dance to portray a shared history.

Books make us think, challenge ideas, give us more information, and encourage curiosity. If a book is acclaimed it can carry on for generations and share its ideas for centuries. If a book is controversial it can spark discussion and encourage people to learn more or seek out answers.

The value of a book is in the mind of the reader. What you consider to be a terrible book could be adored by someone else just as something you might have loved reading can be disdained by another. We each get what we want or what we are looking for from what we read.

Again, and as always, it's important to remember to filter what we read through our own sense of reason. The written word can be dangerous as well as a wonderful and exciting tool for cultivating wisdom. Entire series of books have garnered criticism because of their content.

But criticism breeds curiosity for the wisdom seeker. It's an opportunity to find out why, to get all sides of the story and to proceed with an open mind.

Judy Blume, an American author of dozens of books for young adults, is the most banned author in the USA[i]. Her books touch on everything from bullying to teen sex. One of her challenged titles is "Blubber", the story of bullying and body image as told from the point of view of a 10 year old girl.

"Twilight" was popular enough to be made into film but the entire series has been called into question by a multitude of women's anti-abuse groups around the world[ii].

This controversy sparks discussion, engages the audience and teaches us the importance of questioning what we read, why we read it, who reads it and the value of what was written. Ultimately only you can determine if what you have read had value for you and how that can be measured - if it is indeed something that can be measured at all - but this process is yet another we can use to cultivate our wisdom.

The written word shows us different ways of looking at the world. Whether it's fiction or non-fiction, when we read something written by someone else we are challenged to see the world differently. We may think differently or view the things around us differently because we have read a different perspective or experience from our own.

i   American Library Association (2012) *Most Challenged Authors of the 21st Century*
     http://www.ala.org/advocacy/banned/frequentlychallenged/challengedauthors
ii   Psychology Today Online (2011) *'Relationship Violence in Twilight'*
     http://www.psychologytoday.com/blog/psychologist-the-movies/
     201111/relationship-violence-in-twilight

Reading List:
(These are just a few books that have made me think.)
The Psychology of Happiness by Samuel S. Franklin
Lamb by Christopher Moore
Are You There God? It's Me Margaret by Judy Blume
Breakfast of Champions by Kurt Vonnegut
The Curious Incident of the Dog in the Nighttime by Mark Haddon
The Psychopath Test by Jon Ronson
Doubt by Jennifer Hecht

Add your own!

Author List:

(And these are some authors that I go to for wise tidbits.)

Pema Chodron

Stephen Hawking

The Dalai Lama

Sharon Salzberg

Isaac Asimov

Add your own!

Letting Go &
The Power of Doubt

Have you ever caught yourself getting really worked up about something and then, upon reflection, realising it was something quite silly? Like being really adamant that something be done in a specific way, even if it wouldn't affect the outcome if it was done differently? Or refusing to try something different because it wasn't how you were used to doing things?

It's easy to start taking things too seriously, especially when our egos are involved. Opinions can feel like fact when we hold onto them too tightly. We can become blinded by our opinions, closed minded to different ideas, and therefore shut off from opportunities to cultivate wisdom.

When we practice awareness we run the risk of forming solid opinions which then counteract with our work. As well as questioning received wisdom or universal wisdom, we must also learn to question ourselves. Our own sense of reason changes over time. It's inevitable. The more we learn the more information we have. The more information, the more knowledge, and the more knowledge, the more we have to work with.

One way to combat this is to refrain from applying 'right' and 'wrong' to your thinking process. Remember, opinions are personal beliefs, not fact. Every opinion has merit to the individual who holds it, because an opinion is entirely personal. By practicing letting go of that personal viewpoint we can remain open minded and therefore change our minds.

Being able to change your mind, to admit that something you once believed might not have been helpful or well informed, is a very wise characteristic. I am always impressed when someone puts their hand up to something they've changed their mind about. I have immense respect for them because it takes a lot of guts to change your mind about something.

When you change your mind about something, you're letting go of the need to identify with it by accepting that all things are impermanent. Impermanence is about the inevitability of change. In a world where great importance is put on identity, letting go of a belief can feel like letting go of a bit of yourself. So it definitely takes guts to change your mind.

It is also extremely challenging. Just like action, our thoughts can be habit forming. We can get into the habit of thinking a certain way without realising it. This lack of awareness is another thing that leads to a closed mind. But pay attention to your thoughts and you'll realise very quickly that they really do have a mind of their own.

Thoughts are flighty. A lot of the time we have no control over what will pop into our heads. Practicing awareness (being mindful) of your thoughts to ensure you can remain flexible and open is hard work.

So I have immense respect for those who can let go and remain aware. These are key to cultivating wisdom and neither is easy but both are completely worth it.

We All Have Potential

When cultivating wisdom we must remember that all beings have the same potential for enlightenment. We come from different backgrounds and have different experiences but our ability to cultivate wisdom is inherent, if we choose to access it.

The ego can make us believe that we are better than someone else if we feel that we have figured something out which they haven't. It causes arrogance, self importance and disdain.

To be wise is to recognise that everyone has the same potential and that every path is unique. There is no hierarchy for obtaining enlightenment. It's not a competition.

The cultivation of wisdom is a personal journey, which is why being your own teacher is so important. It would be unwise to judge someone based on where we think they arc on their own path as we cannot know their experience. Any judgement passed about someone else's growth or lack thereof is entirely speculation based upon opinion.

When we cultivate wisdom we must remember that we are only able to determine what is right for us. We can be a judge of our own progress but not that of another.

Good luck, and please feel free to share your stories of cultivating wisdom with me on my blog: www.kaitlynschatch.com or tweet at me: @faunawolf

Genuine Gratitude

This book has been a long time in the works and although I wrote it and also decided - because I'm a bit mad that way - to do the design and layout for it as well, it has not been the work of only one person.

I would like to thank my family for all their support in everything I do. Specifically, I'd like to thank my mum, Shannon, for being so good at her job and believing that you're never too young - or too old - to gain wisdom. I'd also like to thank her for footing the bill for my psychology appointments - which have been essential to my own personal growth and general sanity. I'd like to thank my dad, Julian, for his unwavering faith in my abilities and for always believing in me. My brother, Nick, is also one of my best friends and I want to thank him for sibling rivalry, long winded conversations with multiple tangents and 'foot heat'. And finally, but not by any means least, my sister's from another mister, Kendra and Mara, for imagination, inspiration and lung squeezing hugs.

My gratitude and appreciation to Clare. She has been both an incredible support and a great challenger and without both I wouldn't be half the woman I am today.

I would also like to thank Laura Tosney and Erika Watters for their brilliant editing and feedback, which helped make this book grammatically correct as well as well written.

I have had many teachers, many of whom I've never met, but the most important one in relation to this book being published is Christine Korol, my psychologist and 'most expensive friend'. It's been an amazing journey thanks to her her nudging or blatant butt kicking.

And finally, thank you to all the troublemakers.

Worth a Thought

I don't believe I'm particularly wise. Nothing I've said in this book hasn't been said before and much of the wisdom I've gained has simply been because something I heard made good sense. The following is a list of 'wise tidbits' I've discovered in my own life. It's an incomplete and ever changing list and I invite you to add your own or remove anything that doesn't work for you.

Regret isn't about longing to go back and change something, it's about accepting responsibility for things we've done wrong and promising to surprise ourselves by doing them differently in the future.

If we don't like a situation we can only change our role in it - how we think or feel about it - not the role of anyone else or the situation itself.

We can only help someone as much as they are willing to help themselves.

Let go.

The best revenge is a good life.

To not try is to fail.

We all have unlimited potential.

Everything is impermanent.

You, more than anyone else on the entire planet, deserve your own love and respect.

Holding onto anger or resentment is like holding onto a hot coal and hoping to hit someone with it. You may hit them a few times but you will certainly get burned.

It's never too late to start over again.

The only thing in life that is certain is death. If that is true, and we don't know when death will come, then what is the most important thing right now?

It is our reponsibility to realise our own happiness.

I would rather say I shouldn't have done something than wonder what would have happened if I had.

If you want to do something you'll find a way.

Above the clouds, the sky is always blue.

We do the best we can with what we know.

Don't get angry at a kitten for being a kitten.

Thoughts are like clouds in the sky.

No one does anything because they want to feel worse.

Don't take yourself too seriously.

Smile often. It's better than having frown lines when you're old AND it can really freak people out.

We don't have to like someone to be grateful for them.

Compassion is the ability to see our shared human experience.

You are not alone.

Forgiveness isn't condoning what someone has done but accepting that they didn't know any better.

Be doubtless that you can fail but that you can also succeed.

Be generous.

Stop trying to avoid discomfort.

Embrace groundlessness.

Be curious.

Be playful.

Live with humour.

We can be mindful of the past but remember that the future is wide open. We do not have to repeat things which haven't worked. We can change our future.

Know the rules, inside and out, so you can break them effectively.

Be genuine.

Thank you!